# Garfield rolls on

BY: JIM DAVIS

**BALLANTINE BOOKS · NEW YORK**

Library of Congress Catalog Card Number: 85-90570

ISBN: 0-345-32634-2

Manufactured in the United States of America

First Edition: October 1985

10  9  8  7  6  5  4  3  2  1

RRRRRR

JON'S BEST SHOES!

SOMETIMES ODIE MAKES ME SO ANGRY, I COULD JUST SCREAM

© 1984 United Feature Syndicate, Inc.

ARRRRRGH!

JIM DAVIS   6-3

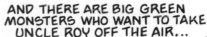

PECK PECK PECK

JIM DAVIS 6·22

STOP PECKING ME WITH THAT RUBBER CHICKEN!

© 1984 United Feature Syndicate, Inc.

AW, LOOK, YOU HURT STRETCH'S FEELINGS

HE BRINGS OUT THE WORST IN ME

POOKY, I WOULD LIKE YOU TO MEET STRETCH, MY RUBBER CHICKEN

JIM DAVIS 6·23

QUITE FRANKLY, POOKY AND STRETCH DON'T HAVE A LOT OF PERSONALITY

© 1984 United Feature Syndicate, Inc.

BUT YOU HAVE TO TRADE OFF SOMETHING WHEN YOU SURROUND YOURSELF WITH GOOD LISTENERS

GARFIELD, I SWEAR YOU'VE DONE EVERYTHING TO ODIE A CAT COULD DO TO A DOG

AU CONTRAIRE

JIM DAVIS

PLINK

6-27

© 1984 United Feature Syndicate, Inc.

NEVER UNDERESTIMATE ME

HEY, ODIE! I FOUND YOUR NOSE!

LET ME PUT IT ON FOR YOU, PAL

SQUIK SQUIK

© 1984 United Feature Syndicate, Inc.

VERY NICE. I LIKE YOU AS A RAT TERRIER

SNIFF

JIM DAVIS

6-28

© 1984 United Feature Syndicate, Inc.

7-8

JIM DAVIS

ALRIGHT, YOU GUYS, GET OUT OF HERE. IT'S ONLY A LITTLE THUNDERSTORM

© 1984 United Feature Syndicate, Inc.

JIM DAVIS 8-26

GUESS WHAT, GARFIELD! WE'RE GOING TO THE FARM THIS WEEK

8-27    JIM DAVIS

WHOOPTY-DOO. GOING TO THE FARM IS LIKE GOING TO THE ZOO...

WHERE THEY EAT EVERYTHING BUT THE CATS

© 1984 United Feature Syndicate, Inc.

DAD! MOM!

JIM DAVIS 8-28

JON BOY!

JONNY!

I WISH THEY'D CALL ME BY MY REAL NAME

YOU'RE RIGHT, DUMMY

© 1984 United Feature Syndicate, Inc.

HEE HEE, THERE'S MORE THAN ONE WAY TO SKIN A CAT

JIM DAVIS 9-14

WHIRRRRR!

HOW PROPHETIC

RATS, GARFIELD FELL ASLEEP IN THE MIDDLE OF THE FLOOR

JIM DAVIS

9-15

HAVE YOU EVER TRIED TO PICK UP A SLEEPING CAT?

IT'S IMPOSSIBLE

9-16 JIM DAVIS

© 1984 United Feature Syndicate, Inc.

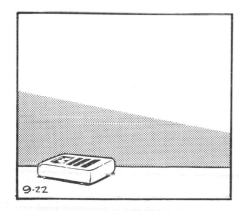

HEY, GARFIELD, WHAT'S ALL THIS JUNK IN YOUR BED?

THIS ISN'T JUNK. THIS IS MY STUFF

I USE THIS BRASS LIZARD TO SCRATCH MY BACK

AND HERE IS SOME EXTRA CAT HAIR FOR YOUR FOOD, AND A DOUBLE CORNCOB THAT IS A FAMILY HEIRLOOM

JIM DAVIS

AND THIS IS MY BEAN-FILLED WHACK-BONK

WHAT DOES THAT DO?

9-23        © 1984 United Feature Syndicate, Inc.

WHACK!

BONK

GOOD MORNING, FOLKS! MY OH MY, IT'S A BEAUTIFUL MONDAY MORNING OUT THERE

10-15

OUR WEATHER RADAR SHOWS CLEAR SKIES WITH NO RAIN IN SIGHT

© 1984 United Feature Syndicate, Inc.

JIM DAVIS

EXCEPT OVER ONE HOUSE IN THE SUBURBS

OUR SATELLITE PICTURE SHOWS CLOUDS OVER THE NORTHEAST, SUNNY SKIES IN THE SOUTHWEST...

10-16

TRAFFIC BACKED UP ON 12TH STREET

© 1984 United Feature Syndicate, Inc.

AND MY LITTLE NIECE, SALLY, PLAYING IN HER SANDBOX IN TEXAS

KIND OF SCARY, ISN'T IT?

JIM DAVIS

CLOUDS ARE SO INTERESTING. I LOVE TO FIND SHAPES IN THEM

THERE'S A CHICKEN CLOUD, AND A HAMBURGER CLOUD, AND A BICYCLE CLOUD

10-19    JIM DAVIS

AND I DO BELIEVE THAT ONE'S A RAIN CLOUD

© 1984 United Feature Syndicate, Inc.

WHAT DO YOU THINK OF MY NEW FRAME, GARFIELD?

10-20

ARRRGH!

© 1984 United Feature Syndicate, Inc.

THANK HEAVENS! FOR A MOMENT THERE I THOUGHT IT WAS A MIRROR

JIM DAVIS

10-21    JIM DAVIS

PUCUCK!

ONE MORE STUNT LIKE THAT AND I'M GOING TO WRING YOUR RUBBER CHICKEN'S NECK!

© 1984 United Feature Syndicate, Inc.

I'M SORRY I SNAPPED AT YOU, GARFIELD. WILL YOU FORGIVE ME?

I FORGIVE YOU

SMACK!

WHAP!

BUT STRETCH DOESN'T!

POO!

KONK!

THE HARDER YOU WORK FOR SOMETHING, THE MORE YOU APPRECIATE IT

© 1984 United Feature Syndicate, Inc.

RATS! THERE'S AN ALLEY FULL OF MEAN GUYS WAITING TO BEAT ME UP!

MAYBE THEY WON'T HURT ME IF I LOOK MEAN, TOO

HEY! IT'S WORKING!

SOMEDAY, I'M GOING TO LEARN PRECISELY WHERE THAT FINE LINE IS, AND I'M NEVER GOING TO CROSS IT AGAIN!

© 1984 United Feature Syndicate, Inc.

12-9

JIM DAVIS

GARFIELD! I'M BACK FROM THE CONVENTION! WHERE ARE YOU, BIG GUY?... GARFIELD?!

12-10

OH, NO! THIS IS TERRIBLE! GARFIELD DIDN'T GET LOCKED OUT OR ANYTHING, DID HE, ODIE?

YUP

© 1984 United Feature Syndicate, Inc.

JIM DAVIS

HELLO, GARFIELD

DO I KNOW YOU?

© 1984 United Feature Syndicate, Inc.

LET ME GIVE YOU A HINT... SIT UP STRAIGHT. DON'T TALK WITH YOUR MOUTH FULL. WAKE UP, SLEEPYHEAD

12-11

JIM DAVIS

MOM!

JIM DAVIS

12-16

© 1984 United Feature Syndicate, Inc. 12-28

© 12-29

© 1984 United Feature Syndicate, Inc.